First Harvests
(A Collection of Poems from Nkongho-Mboland)

Edited by

Fonkeng E.F
& Fonsah E.G.

Langaa Research & Publishing CIG
Mankon, Bamenda

Publisher:

Langaa RPCIG
Langaa Research & Publishing Common Initiative Group
P.O. Box 902 Mankon
Bamenda
North West Region
Cameroon
Langaagrp@gmail.com
www.langaa-rpcig.net

Distributed in and outside N. America by African Books Collective
orders@africanbookscollective.com
www.africanbookcollective.com

ISBN: 9956-728-04-7

DISCLAIMER
All views expressed in this publication are those of the author and do not necessarily reflect the views of Langaa RPCIG.

Dedication

Student, friend, father, teacher, counselor, intellectual, philanthropist
All rolled into one, as no boundary did your life establish but to all things good
Of a conscience and moral probity beyond reproach.
A life inspired by a vision of enrichment of the human mind and the building of the complete human being as the antidote to prevailing human and societal problems.

Many things and tasks in a full life
Catholic parish leader,
Trade unionist, as Secretary of the National Teachers' Union of Cameroon
Politician (when the word was clean), and the testimony of a kindred spirit offered by the people of Fontem
Who, in1963, would choose this 'stranger' as their candidate-representative for the West Cameroon Parliament

Above all, a career teacher - your calling, vocation and passion, for over forty years.
The loose and tenuous kinship with financial reward or personal aggrandizement of no concern to you
Would not jump ship, as many contemporaries, to the lucrative field of 'government teacher'
The pressures from friends and family notwithstanding

Happy, it seemed all along, to work for a pittance till the drawing of the curtain
Happier still, fighting the curse of illiteracy from wherever it reared its head.

At many stations too, you stopped, on this journey: Mbetta, Fontem, Soppo, Mutengene, Kumba…
Bringing out of this man the *summum bonum*
Through your house and hands, and under your wings the philanthropist in you,
would ensure an education for willing but hard-pressed kids,
their tuition in toe at the slightest sign of parental inability to pay
Man of modest formal education, yourself
From under your protective wings would fly out eventual doctors, professors, researchers….
We seek to understand your depth, Mboh
Opened your home to children and parents seeking help with life's sundry problems.

Counselor
Born in July 1927, of a modest background, modestly you would strive to live
Billed for succession, as the eldest son to the village chief
You would defer to your younger brother, when the time came, to ascend to the throne
A precedent, thus, you created in the land through this humbly mighty act

And who but a trailblazer and thinker outside the box to enroll a son into St.Theresia all-girls school, Kumba?
Thereby singlehandedly putting an end to the practice of single sex schools

What but a trailblazing act your pluri-denominational Big Ten
group for the cause of education across Meme!
A true testimony of your Intellectual credential

Remiss we would be if we did not call to mind and cherish
your holding court among the people,
As you would draw on all the rich proverbs and wisdom
sayings of Lekongho -
 the only language you are credited to ever speaking to your
children! -
As you explained the rewards of education, and imparted
your wisdom on life

A deserved State medal later in life does not even begin to
pay our debt to you
Bigger than the Ngungu, above which you tower
We are all, language, sex and creed inconsequential
A little richer in virtues and our station in life
Because of You, Mboh

For you, dear friend, father, teacher, counselor, worker,
philanthropist….
The ancestors have created a soft spot!
For you to lay back, and marvel
'Did I do all these things?'
Yes, you did – and more!

Table of Contents

Introduction

Welcome to the first ever poetry collection by a few sons and daughters of Nkongho-Mbo origin. It is not so much the origin of the authors as it is the fact that this outcome is actually a 'side-show' to a much more ambitious project we have been contemplating for some time now: a comprehensive title on the Nkongho-Mbos.

The Nkongho-Mbos are a sub-group of the Mbo ethnic group of Cameroon, Central Africa, on whom not much has been written and/or published. The reasons for this we ignore, but we figure it has much to do with the smallness of the group, compared to the others, and its consequent absence of influence on the aggregate political, social and economic structure and system of the country.

So, as you wait for that first comprehensive title on the Mbos, we trust you will enjoy these verses which, as one of the authors puts it, are no more than "expressions of impressions" on a variety of local and universal phenomena and states of being.

Part 1 - Tributes

Acha Tugi

Rising and falling
Through a dusty, rocky and tortuous road
and landscape
And there in sight is Acha Tugi

Pockets of man-made forest
Cypress and eucalyptus grace open grass fields
Dance to the quick succession of rhythms
Gentle and violent – of the morning harmattan

Red-roofed structures
Architecture embellished
In simple, couleur locale, sublime
Inside, a hospital so real

A friendly and brotherly staff
In whom simplicity reigns supreme
And of a devotion truly zealous

Each morning they trickle in, the sick
In tens, hundreds, long faces they pull
Long faces they pull
Aggrieved by tribulations of every name

Then, at the end of a sojourn
Long or short
Homeward-bound they set
Faces beaming with smiles

For true solace
Bodily and in spirit

They found and got in Acha Tugi
Home away from home

Fonkeng E.f.

Invisible Gift

Here I stand alone, in the wilderness
Staring at what looks like your tomb
Unable to determine where to lay the flowers
For that I beg for your forgiveness

I wonder and I question
Why, mostly, I'm never around on this day
Always in some transcontinental flight
Thinking of you and weeping in silence

I thought I'd come around this time
So close as to feel your presence
So you would help me locate the exact spot
Before I jet off on yet another long-distance one

Intentional or coincidental, I know not
Despite my philosophizing and spiritualizing
Still, I thank you for the gift you offered a few days after the
burial
Its twenty-four years today; how you looked gorgeous in that
burial suit!

I never told a soul about the gift, except one
An elder warned me never to mention it again
As some powerful spirit might snatch it away from me

Sorry if I did offend you. I was only sixteen then
Again, I thank you, Dad, I love you.

Esendugue Greg Fonsah

Little and Big Things

They had a bit, a tiny little bit
Just an infinitesimal fraction of the whole
They were humorous, friendly and liked by everyone
They wished they had a little more

They had a bit, a tiny little stolen bit
No one bothered to find out the source
'Cause it was little, so little to arouse suspicions
It gave them happiness and pleasure

They had a little bit, which was snatched away by time
It brought them unhappiness, moodiness, and pain
They realized the little bit was more than enough if rationed
They only had to stretch existence of the tiny little bit

They had a little bit, a tiny little unattended bit
The owners suspected a tiny little portion of their fortress
was missing
It was too tiny to be bothered with for those who had in
abundance
But, it was a treasure for those who lay stake to attain the tiny
bit.

Esendugue Greg Fonsah

For the Sake of Principle

Da man
Pah Long Trosa
Mbo lawyer
Pocket lawyer

Names he's bagged in abundance
A testimony of the awe
He's never ceased to create
But of all, never 'been loved.

For a strict and ascetic life
Probity in public and private realm
An extreme rigid consistency
Pursues he straightforwardly

Tall and lanky
Religiously clean-shaven
Assuredly he gently walks
Need still he sees not
Although well an octogenarian
For a third leg

Fonkeng E.f.

Treasure

I can only have a bit
For someone else has it big
I wish I could get it all
I know I can't for sure

My bit is however cherished
As without it I could perish
Even though I loose the big
I will always have this bit

My bit is not a whole
But is printed in my soul
I take it everywhere I go
And with it make my being whole

My heart aches seeing so much
For the uncertainty without much
But I hang on to my bit
For the consolation I need

Forsac D. Etogokwe

Meditation

I thank you for all the blessings
For the spiritual doctrine and philosophy
For the departing gift
I took your advice – everything you said has come true

You taught me that hard work assures a future
Indeed, it has brightened mine
Everything I dreamed, I have achieved
Education, fame, good job, self-esteem and self-actualization

We now have more than we ever before
Mom is still alive, old but strong, healthy and kicking
We cannot use the things we have by ourselves
We wish you were around to share them with us

We have a son who looks just like you
He is as handsome as you
He is as stubborn as you
He is as smart as you

Could it be that you came back just like you said?
Should I agonize then over your share of the cake?
He, who we named after you has it big
Could this be a mere coincidence?

Please explain this to me like in the past, would you?
I'd also want to know your whereabouts presently
Are you with our Ancestors, where?
I miss you so very much.

Esendugue Greg Fonsah

First Christmas

He was just four months old
Mom and Dad were very poor
She won't miss the church service for the world
Although she had no cloth for her two children

He was only four months old
Mama insisted to honor the birth of Christ
Mama wrapped him up in a torn rag
His sister had on an old dress

As Mama ascended the staircase to the church
She missed her steps and fell
Her four month old was crying
His sister was bleeding to death

Thirty-eight years later, this day was different
The four month old now had more than one person could
possibly have
Friends of every horizon were invited to a lavish candlelight
buffet
They drank the most expensive wine and champagne

Esendugue Greg Fonsah

Tribute
(To my dear friend Ephraim)

When the story of a life is written
It will say I found a friend in you
Sometimes we sing of the friendship we have
Ours though not sung is real ad true
Thank you for your friendship

Some hearts must train to be good and loving
Some minds must train to be open and receptive
Some spirits must evolve to be joyful and illuminating
You need not train, you need not evolve
These gifts were yours at birth

Convention commands the young will learn from the old
Yet from you I have learnt a lot
Uplifting qualities rare to find in one
A glowing heart overflowing with love
You have them all and so much more

The mystery of life unfolds through time
We know not where it will lead us
As long as it is in my power to do
I will always hold you dear and true
Thank you for your friendship

Forsac Amatus

Ako Aya

And so rolls the life of a fighter
Short, yet not sweet
Painful to his followers
Your loss, reason we have to mourn
'Cause in it we find not a surrogate

A cause so valiant you alone championed
Where others bow out unceremoniously
That freedom is not received on a golden platter...
But is won battle after battle
That truth is not found under the king's boots
But is borne out of the 'market place of ideas'
A meaning of life you fought to portray
That man does not live by bread alone

Yonder, with our ancestors, you're gone to rest
Leaving us orphans for ourselves, to nest
Still, the courageous leadership
Synonymous with your name
Is more than enough inspiration and incitement
A truly evergreen homage to you to pay
In vigilance and service

So rolls the life of a fighter

Fonkeng E.f.

Childhood

The innocence I cannot express
The feelings, I do remember
A Golden Age of Being, it was
A time of adventure and naivety, it was
So precious yet so ephemeral
T'was yesterday

Youth is Paradise
It is trusting absolutely
It is purity of heart
A heart divine, well, like God's

What happened to Paradise?
Well, we grew and so did the weeds around us
We became contaminated
No longer innocent
No longer pure
No longer adventurous
No longer naïve
Hell has taken over
We beg only, for forgiveness

Today, we sit and yearn
Yearn for your Return
Lessons ingrained cannot be forgotten
We struggle to return to hope
And there is hope
Hope, to return to innocence
Hope, if we do right
Hope, through our children
To relive the times

Times, where we too were once free

Fonge T. Tobias

Mother

Dearest, sweetest mother
Incomparable one
Most cherished possession ever
Is it true you're gone?

Warm, kind and loving
Best counselor ever
What pay for all the mighty deeds?
Be absent to bid farewell!

Brave warrior who would not bend
To sickness and worldly tribulations
The man-eaters may rejoice
But who lasts forever?

It grieves to see you depart – so soon
Mother, for whom did I chase the golden fleece?
I thought I could reciprocate your love
And assuage your sufferings

No! The one who gives and takes
Has taken as He gave
In the wilderness I stand, arms outstretched
Seeking to touch yours

Mother, I hope and pray and believe

With your undaunting faith
Your journey will come to a sweet end
Did it not begin on Christmas day?

Ahead you're gone, preparing the way
With them before you watch over me
When finally I come
Never no more shall we ever part

Fonkeng E.f.

The Birocol Song

Brotherhood, Rectitude, Service
From you, these our triple credo
Implanted in the fresh minds we were
Fresh as the nearby Tole tea we daily drank
Under the cold, breezy yet fresh and sweet
Slopes of Soppo – below the Mount Fako

Mens sana in corpore sano
Every sixteen hours in a workful day
We read history, *econs*, maths, music and all
The unique excitement of it all – Latin!
We recited *Mentor* and *Cicero*
In Soppo we sang and danced, played and prayed

In self-help our own land we farmed
Washed our dishes and cleaned our hostels
Life we 'entered' through the Club Spirit
To uphold we pledge the lesson in all these
Laborare est Orare
That to work is to pray

Birocol, my Alma Mater ever dear
To the revered memory of a brave Father
O! the Rev'rend Bishop Peter Rogan
Moulding the tender hearts to temples of
Brotherhood, Rectitude and Service
For always with you we shall be

Fonkeng, E.f.

Missing You

I wish it were just us
I wish it were in Nature plain
I wish it were in the jungle, with waterfalls
I wish it were in the heart of a banana plantation

It's got to be the long awaited reunion and moments spent
together
It's got to be the last letter as the distance between us widens
Gosh – all the wishes were miraculously fulfilled
And, I miss them

I also miss the expensive bad habits
Which I never tolerated
But I did, this time around
I miss the angelic smiles that brought sunshine in our family
and being

I miss the telepathic attitude and the running downstairs
To deliver the most appealing and welcoming kisses

And the red carpeted hugs that facilitated our movement upstairs
I miss the care and concern that brought humor
And kept the whole atmosphere alive and easy to dwell on

I miss the ebony straight hair
The massages, the smooth and gentle touches
That added flavor in our love life, and above all
I miss you very much

Esendugue Greg Fonsah

Part II - Encounters

Miss Ngeme

Her long silky dark hair rose majestically
Then her black slant eyes irradiated like the full moon
Everyone froze, stared admiringly
Trying to guess – Miss Ngeme?
Miss Ngeme! the thought ran through several minds

The door opened slowly, the stares persisted
A well-shaped pair of legs touched the ground, softly
On them, an evenly trimmed sculpture of a body
Sending an exciting signal to all who watched with anxiety
Must be Miss Ngeme, someone in the crowd whispered

The most gorgeous creature ever seen around here
A vibrant smile, that took away everyone's breath
Embedded in a short, black dress that exhibited the equitable
Dimensions of each body part, rendering her even prettier
Was she a fairy, Miss Ngeme, or both?

The soft and seductive voice blended in with her beauty-
power
Her slim layered moistened lips were irresistible
Miss Ngeme, indeed, named after the village that lies
Between the Atlantic Ocean and the foot of Mount Fako

Esendugue Greg Fonsah

Feelings

You've burst open my ball of inspiration
It comes flowing like lava from an erupting mountain
With no one but you to appreciate its content
No one but you to understand

Illness comes into my way
And reduces my level of concentration
But I pray to God and fight hard
To face up to the challenges you set
And through success make us two proud

Watching *Titanic* brings back good memories
And I re-live every moment of it
Two who would steal any extra minute to be together
I never knew love could be this strong

Forsac D. Etogokwe

Love

What is your name?
Are you affection, passion?
Infatuation, enchantment?
Emotion, fondness?
Or is it respect, regard?
Appreciation and devotion?
What is it?

Should we use your name when touched?
When we experience emotional fulfillment?

Where is your boundary?
Should we use your name for the spiritual?
And the physical?

Or is it fair to you to use your name
To describe notions?
Is your name that meaningless?
I yearn to know your boundary
If you have no boundary
I revere you not
No doubt, your name is such commonplace

Fonge T. Tobias

Not Hate

It was not hatred
Nor was it dislike
Though one gave it
To be known that
It was one of the two

Of admiration and attraction
It might have been one
 Not hatred, not even dislike

Some gestures were forgivable
As they were coy or pompous
But one could not hate
Not dislike for that

A fair thing in complexion

Fair in cut and build
Fair in nurture and habit
Nothing could one fairer find
After long, long a sojourn

Fombin P.F.

Hurt

I hurt like I've never known
My heart aches, my soul weeps
My tongue dries up
My very foundation is shaken
My concentration weakens
My vision blurs
Regrets fill my heart

I hurt to think about it
I hurt and can't measure
I hurt like you'd never know
For you are not in me

How did I get so hurt
Why did I allow it
How can I manage it
It hurt me more than I can say

I'll figure out the source
I'll keep away from it
I can't manage another
I'll crash under its weight

I hurt against my will
I pray to God it stops
I weep to soothe my hurt
I weep to sleep off my hurt

Forsac D. Etogokwe

The Distance between our Bond

They waited for me in the office
They stood up, chanting the birthday song
Surprise and shock, I walked right through the singing crowd
I did not remember my birthday

My boss rushed into my file to verify
My colleagues paused as I paraded to my desk
They watched with astonishment
I suspected something was amiss, and ooops

September 15, I exclaimed
Humh, my American colleagues answered
"What's wrong with you, man?"
Don't you Africans have birthdays?

Sorry, I'm just not used to it
I never had one before
What do you mean? We can't understand
You Africans don't have birthdays?

We do if you're uppity
I had my birthday at my birth
I'm still waiting my death day.

My truth shocked them
And this, the distance between our bond

Esendugue Greg Fonsah

Love Daze

She lay still in a transparent coffin
All the beauty gone despite the make-up
Alas, the photograph on the wall looked real
Sending out magnetic vibrations
As those she cared most could feel the presence

Then she stood next to the picture on the wall
A semblance of her living state
But for her complexion and her name
And the glasses, a mere camouflage, of course
She turned 180 degrees, our eyes met
She was prettier than ever

For a moment, I was dumbfounded
Her magnetic signals sent a chill down my spine
And the message was gradually transmitted
She completely reverted the terms of our friendship
Impossible it was to resist the temptation
Even though we both were engaged and she, dead, in my
mind

The sensations were too good to be true
The were scary, and even after a decade of friendship
Her hot smiles, touches, kisses could melt even a steel bar

Her body cliffs, secluded valleys and her love lava stretching
to Seme Beach
Was she a ghost or fairy? Was she simply my imagination?
Or was this reincarnation?

Esendugue Greg Fonsah

Mile Six Beach

We hit the highway heading South West
As we listened to Nat King Cole's best hits
Our destination, Mile Six Beach
In the heart of the rainy season

Somehow, the weather was bright with sunshine
The perfect blue sky, with patches of white clouds
Some resembled clusters of Fako ready to erupt
Others, like parading dinosaurs

The ocean waves slammed against the huge clustered shores
of volcanic rock
The mangrove trees swayed sideways to the music of the
wind
The kingfishers flew all about singing songs of the land
While hunting fishes by the shore

On the beach, a sampling of every nationality
A United Nations in the heart of Africa
Some wore dental floss, boxing shorts or braces
Others in tempting bikini stripes
Lovers moved in pairs, and families in groups
Each subgroup admiring the other

Everyone was having fun, enjoying the weather
No one talked of racism, HIV, wars or death
This corner of the Atlantic was absolute beauty and sanity
This day at Mile 6 Beach
In the heart of my Africa

Esendugue Greg Fonsah

The View from Ngeme Village

A bunch of innocent kids, naked and in rags, march down a
ramp
Leading straight into the mighty Atlantic
They anchor the wooden one-seater of a canoe
As ocean currents pound against the volcanic rocks

Coconut trees dance to the music of the wind
A village fisherman pulls in as the children evaluate his day's
catch
Upstream, adults take their bath
Where spring water drains into the salty ocean
Who is crossing the road, or starring, crosses not their minds

Whites and uppity Africans sit in buckaroos well-kept
Sipping tea, coffee, or whatever, on this ocean corner
Watching the Africans as they swim and bathe
Enjoying the nearby Fako, the Harmattan – the nakedness
before them, too

It is tough to swim the gulf between the two worlds
One marked by extreme deprivation and hardship

The other full of extreme wealth, gluttony and hedonism
How come this stark disparity demarcated today by such a
fine line?

Esendugue Greg Fonsah

The Cat and the Dog

The Siamese Cat had half a dozen beautiful kittens
She was young, strong and hard working single mother cat
Life was fun and perfect as the kittens grew up
Because the young mother cat provided all they needed

Some of the mature kittens began bearing their own siblings
The kittens and grand-kits were not hardworking and
industrious
Unfortunately the grandmother cat was growing older ad
weaker faster
She could no longer support her half dozen kittens and a
third of a dozen grand kits

Life became unpleasant and frustrating
One of the half dozen kittens was in fact pretty, hardworking,
intelligent
And was appreciated by all the family members
She was a role model to her sisters and neighboring kittens

The entire family looked up to her for their needs
Since the mother cat could no longer improvise
But she was still young, unprepared to assume parental
responsibilities
And even unable to support herself

Since she was the only hope
She stretched herself
A little too far
So as to meet these unfair demands

Her best friend was a bourgeois German Shepherd dog who lived
Virtually on principles and superior ethical values
He provided her moral, philosophical and ethical lessons
Because he admired her beauty, suppleness, agility and indifference

Just as she started getting to appreciate the German Shepherd's life-style and philosophy
Her family situation worsened and everyone looked up to her for physiological needs
The German shepherd could not provide the kind of
Assistance needed by her family for moral ad ethical reasons

She was helpless and had no one to turn to
She could not understand why her German shepherd friend was so
Moralistically and ethically oriented
Fortunately, a coyote dog volunteered his services with strings attached

Although the offer was too good to be refused, the pretty cat still admired,
Respected and was too attached to the German Shepherd
She was caught between good and evil, reputation and family
The German Shepherd and the coyote dog; but she strived to satisfy all

The pretty cat lost the admiration and protection
provided by the German shepherd
She also lost the appreciation and role model status
From the pet animals in their community and neighborhood

Because she was no longer special and indifferent
 From her sisters nor the neighboring kittens
She was vulnerable, indeed, worried
And uncomfortable with the whole ordeal

Who is to blame?
The pretty cat?
 The family?
 The German Shepherd or the Coyote dog?

Esendugue Greg Fonsah

The Sex Controversy

The weaker sex!
Sits on the stronger sex
Controls its thoughts and actions
The source of its follies and passions
They call it the weaker sex

The weaker sex!
The overblown creation
That is this generation's song
The imagined captive of a sex
They call the stronger sex

The weaker sex
Guided by those whose way of life it guides
Those cocooned in a misguided equation
That shortage of physical might
Equals a weaker sex

The weaker sex
Liberated for all time has been
Didn't you hear it said, alas
What a man can do a woman can?
Maybe the stronger sex?

Nay, the equal sex
Powerless under its master
Powerful over its slave
Slow, silent, top-down and bottom up
Yes, t'is the equal sex

Fonkeng E.f.

Na Man Kill Man

A broad smile he gloated
Through tobacco-brown set of teeth
As he showed the seat, in front of him
Preparing for the kill

"Mister Man, it's my considered opinion
Fifteen mistakes on the test weigh too heavy
Your inefficiency to conceal
"No, no protests!
Good luck elsewhere!"

The sexy busts protruded
Through a transparent silky white
In his seat he shuffled uneasily
 His eyes undressing her
As he plotted another night kill

"Miss, it's my considered opinion
Fifty errors ain't too plenty
To deny you the job
Your co-operation
Last night was marvelous."

Fonkeng E.f.

My Way, Your way

We were best of friends
Despite our mutual admiration
And a desire to go the distance
There were social constraints

We were best friends
Your departure plans punctured our hearts
The fear of losing each other lingered on
There were professional constraints

All contact was severed with your departure
We traded blame for the long silence
without striving to break the ice
Your letter reached a year and half later

The break intensified, deviated interests,
values and responsibilities
Waning our mutual feelings for each other
Constraining our friendship

Esendugue Greg Fonsah

Know Thyself

Know thyself, my friend
Know thyself
Know what lies within
Not without
Put something in thy head
Not on it

To understand others
Is to understand thyself
To know the world
Begins with thyself
Thyself is all you got
Let it rot, not

Fonge T. Tobias

The Captive

Caught betwixt and bewitched
In a state of a double man
Seeking vainly the balance
Between a civilization of terror
Of silver-gilt savagery and violence
And a civilization in meek defense and servitude
Seeking to cast yonder his identity
And find it
Wanting his independence
But accepting dependence

The Captive
East or West for him?
Is home really the best?
Or *is the monkey right?*
Does greatness lie in the things
Of the *mukala?*

Does the sun
Rise in the West
And set in the East?
He looks South, the Captive
Shunning the blinding rays
Now in the North – to which he moves

Aware of the Cripple's dignity, he is
Yet learns to reject that which is his
Albeit the merits in which he sees
And that the shark's back's not a home

A two-faced man
Tormented by the worry of indecision
Is his 'bad' worse than their 'good'
Is their 'good' better than his 'bad'
Hard to find the balance – the answer

Fonkeng, E.f.

Children

What source of joy to those who have
What anxiety to those who wait
What disillusionment to those who don't have
What delicate task to those who must bring them up
What fulfillment in those who succeed
What pain to those who do not

Are they really worth the trouble?
Do they really spice up life?
Do they guarantee a peaceful end?
Do they guarantee happiness?

Forsac D. Etogokwe

In Lighter Moments

Commotion, rowdiness
Eyes up, right, left
And up, right and left again
Catchin' glimpses
Catchin' whole images
As they straddle past
A mother popcorn here
A Cinderella there
To a mixed display
Of admiration and consternation

Then up, down
Up and down again
Gesticulating
Exchanging sordities here
Uttering provocations there
They seem to must
As these struggle past
It's just a moment in an amphitheatre
Of the Yaounde University

Fonkeng E.f.

Part III - Loss

My Best Friend

She was really my best friend
Slim sculptured-like body with elegant neck structure
That matched her long dark hair and well defined cheekbones
Although a mother of a baby girl
She desperately wanted another child
Irrespective of the gender

Then came the good news, she was pregnant
She couldn't wait to see her newborn baby
All discussions centered on the baby
And as the pregnancy approached its term
She'd call me on the phone and talk about her baby
'Cause she had no true trusted friend but me

She confided secrets, joys and mishaps
I listened with abundant patience
Then, one day an early morning phone call
She and the baby were gone – just hours after delivering
She was my best friend
May her soul rest in perfect peace

Esendugue Greg Fonsah

Acada

What does it matter
If the people
With empty bowels
Still shouts can utter?

What does it matter
If the people
Still no word can utter
Even with stuffed mouths

Does it matter
 If after our 'breakthroughs"
And theories, them all
 Stand still we do?

Unfree still
Brutish estranged?
The *acada* battle
For power
Over moeurs
For the self

Fonkeng E.f.

Na Wanda

Kontri pikin them, na weti noh?
Which kana fashion dis, dis time so?
Wuna say na nyong people life, eh?
Ah seeee

40

So so waka waka
Woman oh
So so waka
Nyong boy, oh
So so waka

Dey say weti man do, woman fit do'am
(Ah ah! You noh see dey di wear trosa and shet)?
Tif sef, nyong girl dey inside now

Waka waka
Nyong boy and nyong girl
Tif tif sef
Na all dem
Dey inside oh

Ah seh kontri people, na weti?
Which kana world we dey inside dis time?
Wuna say na nyong people fashion, eh?

Ah seeee
Waka waka (na all dem)
Tif tif (na all dem)
Jealousy (na all dem)
Kongosai (na all dem)
Troway pikin for latrine (na wanda)
Moov beleh (na wanda)

Fonkeng E.f.

The Great Hawk

They put him inside a great hawk
I wept and begged them to let me too in
But they refused my awful pleadings

They refused all of them coldly
Then the hawk made a great noise
It's wings revolved dreadfully fast
Displacing huge volumes of air

Wonderfully huge volumes of air
The hawk raced fast along the ground
Like an immense ostrich
Making a deafening noise all around

All around and wide away
The hawk raced bearing away
My son in its hawling bowels
Oh where was it going with my son?

Flying away with a corpse of my son
Tears gushed freely from my eyes
I wondered how I would live henceforth
That son was my existence all and all

That son was all my hope
For sometime the hawk disappeared
Running very fast along the ground
Then it reappeared flying lowly past

Flying past us with a great noise
Far away it looked so very small

Like a flying insect
It flew fast and was now so small

Now so irreparably gone
Oh my son, oh my beloved son
What have men done with my son?
Oh my son, my only eye, my all

Fombin P.F.

Anxiety

The anxiety of waiting lengthens my nights
And renders my days meaningless
My mouth loses its taste buds
And food is reduced to chaff

The days are counted backwards
As the clock ticks the minutes away
How long have I to wait
For the spice of my life to be restored?

Forsac D. Etogokwe

Brain Drain

The great march ex-Africa
Will they become the prodigal children?
As the wait continues
For the back to Africa march to commence

On their own and
Independent of their volition, they exit
The victims of their conscience - their crime
Africa's unwanted ambassadors
Africa's most wanted manpower

Wither Africa?
As your children roam the globe
In search of silver and gold
Of the good things of life'
Which you have in abundance?
You bleed on
From the trauma of antidevelopment
And they, discriminated
Their color, their crime

In their stead have stepped the 'specialists'
The fruit of the white-is-right mentality
The seed of the *Iroko*
Whose falling branches push young bananas
And upset roots, pull young plants
Leading all to their graves – its foundation!
Whither Africa?

Even the monkey does know
The shark's back's not a home

So whence stops the mass suicide
Africa, when?

Fonkeng E.f.

Unholy Trinity

They came in strides unlike, minds alike
Discovered and plundered
The Missionary, the military and the monetary - managers
Mercenaries, playing for a common cause
To colonize, to christianize –
Nay, to civilize

The rape of land and mind
They sweet-talked and code-talked
With their Missionary
Browbeat into submission
With their military
Flabbergasted and enticed
With their money

The rape of land and mind
The managers –
With a queer mannerism or two
Managing it all well
Their mode, their code, esoteric
Understood by them alone
Our fate we now understand

The rape of the land and mind
Like a rat's bite

Our common grief
Their common harvest
Continues to spread, in
Five hundred fold and counting
The rape of land and mind

Fonkeng E.f.

To Ngwenka

Is this you, Ngwenka
That was once expansive, fresh water pool?
Is this you that was though very calm, mighty and fair?
Is this you that daily opened your bosom to us visitors?

The heat-bathed and mentally tired school children
Came tumbling down the steep slopes every noon
And in a split second tore off their tattered clothes
To dive into your dark fresh and inviting bosom

For hours, the naked boys, big and small
(Their things dancing to the tuneful music of innocence)
Exhausted their creative talent in games of all sorts
Exploring your darksome wide opened chambers

Is this you Ngwenka
Become so aridly barren?
The rugged underwater rocks
Now over-looking
The little patch of you?

You lie on your cradle
Like an ant
Lying on an
Elephant's
Bed

Fombin P.F.

Crocodile Tears

Roam like a roving ghost
In search of a fairy tale castle
Only a shadow of my past glory
I now seem to must

Curse unto my strangler
Seventy-fold to my offspring
Who at akimbo stood and would not kill
This venomous Mamba, in self-defense

You drink from my poisoned fountain
You sway off the pendulum's pivot
(as) you slumber in your dance still
And inter me, half-alive

No sting did you attempt to dare
As the Hawk continues the chicken swoop
Slowly and surely, one by one
And now you shed tears for *Osagyefo*?

Fonkeng E.f.

Bandit Hymn

Singing the bandit song
Everyday
Seems like life's bandwagon
That helter shelter to catch
The race we enter, anyway

Team mates, opponents, together
Singing, playing and marching
To the bandit song

Right notes, wrong chords
T'is everyone's song
The bandit song
Playing the song of time
Each and all
Yet blaming it on time
T'is become so hard, the quest
And money-find is rat race

Dancing to the bandit song
Knows no generation gap
Family and stranger
Parent and child
The sick and the strong
Each versus the other
In the chorus of the one and only song

The struggle continues
Money is the way
Did you hear that?

That life so strong
Office and street robbery
Mental and physical corruption
Positive Nos and negative Yeses
With conscience or with none
For money – for the self
We are singing, playing and marching
To the bandit song

Fonkeng E.f.

Ebamu of the Hills

She came from the hills every morning
And she came red as unripe plums
I saw her when she well could carry a kenja*
And saw she was a bright as the sun

Ebamu came every morning with the sun
And every eye that saw her gave a sigh
As she came down from the hills
Oh! Ebamu of the tall hills of Ngientu

From hill to hill and from valley to valley
From hut to hut and from compound to compound
The name Ebamu was mentioned by all
The melting Ebamu of the green hill of Ngientu

If it was work, Ebamu was smart
If a dance, her shoulders quivered
As if there was not a bone in her

49

Ah! Ebamu was a child, a child
Everyone and everything loved Ebamu
Oh Ebamu! The red Ebamu of the hills
The melting Ebamu of the tall green Hills
Everything loved her and…the Leopard too

Down, downhill at sunrise that day
A sharp cry rang through the valley
Everyone and everything came to seek Ebamu
But woe! They found the red blood of Ebamu

For seven days they searched and searched
For seven full days they moaned and moaned
For seven full days they drummed and danced
And for seven full days Ebamu was not seen

Oh, the melting Ebamu of the green hill
Ah, the sunny Ebamu of the tall hill
Weh, the beloved Ebamu of Ngientu
Ugh, the red Ebamu of the Leopard

Fombin P.F.

Psycho-Vibration

Echoes of drum beats vibrated in my ears
Then a deep voice whispered
He's had an accident
It was like a dream

My feet dragged and my head grew larger
The voice pounded right into my head again and again
Suddenly, I regained consciousness and followed the message
Running as fast as I could through the crowded street

That must be his son
Whispered another strange voice from the crowd
I felt a repugnant vibration as I ran, ran, ran
Arriving at what looked like the accident scene

Another echo: hospital, hospital, and hospital
To the nearest hospital, I ran and ran and ran
He was bleeding to death
Doctor, call my son please, he cried out in agony

Here he is, said the Doctor
Son, I won't be alive before dawn
He died at midnight
I loved him, I did

Esendugue Greg Fonsah

Mu-ngang

Some hate you, others like you, anyway
For what you did and can do, they say
Omnipotent and present you
Hope they forget not
You're but a double-edged spear
At the mercy of the marksman

We didn't, when we could use, you
To smite and smash the witch
The fault's not in you
Omnipotent and present you
But in we who have used you
To smite and smash kith and kin

Fonkeng E.f.

The Accident

It was raining cats and dogs
A suspicion ran through my mind
An immediate farm inspection came to mind
My instinct was rendered exact
The farm was flooded

It was raining cats and dogs
My truck got stuck in the mud while searching
The side rear mirrors and back windshield were dampened
With persistent inferior visibility in and out
As I searched for a rescue drainage team

It was raining cats and dogs
When an unpleasant noise was heard behind my truck
The cry of a vigorous sword sucker with her mother being
crushed
The mother plant was carrying a beautiful five weeks old
Ten-hand bunch with a blue ribbon on it

It was raining cats and dogs
As I pruned the dead sword sucker, chopped her mother and
fruit
I was "water soaked" all through the operation
It was agonizing and painful to execute the pruning and
chopping exercise
To save my asphyxiating banana

Esendugue Greg Fonsah

The Night Train

Passenger-victims, sturdy and frail
Looks menacing, and meek
Like tigers defending territory
Or lamb seeking out survival

Cargo, under and around them
Women, babies glued to their backs, crying
All praying – for some salvation

Under the squelching sun and into the moonlight
They must wait, fighting out these awful hours
Families bid multiple farewells

Finally, the monstrous metallic snake shows up
It's a mad battle to board
Madder still the next phase – for seats

A sudden deafening horn follows another eternity
The huge thing jerks forward
Dark smoke engulfs the pristine atmosphere

Then, an angry and nonchalant loudspeaker scream
The train will be leaving in five minutes
No one heeds, for it never does

The boarding battle, now a penultimate war
For seats – any kind of space
This is Existence, here and now

Again, the monster jerks forward. And stops!
Sending its screaming human cargo

Bumping into metal, livestock and cargo

Just the start to a three-hundred mile, twelve-hour nightmare
With thieves, watchful for a loose wallet, or anything
As 'travelers' sell "their" seats to the frail and desperate

Vendors galore peddling everything and anything
Foodstuffs, water, alcohol, clothes, gadgets, open and concealed
Squeezing their way through human and other cargo, in the dark

Tonight there are fifteen aged wagons, packed full
Ninety-nine sitting, nine ninety-nine standing
Suffering and smiling, the popular song says

As this monster creaks and crawls from side to side
And passengers mimic, in spite of themselves, the dance
Of the night train on the Douala-Yaounde line

Fonkeng E.f.

Out of Sight

Like a storm you came into my life
Shaking the building to its very foundation
Re-arranging all the furniture to your taste
A taste even more pleasing to me

The ball has been set rolling
God helps the direction it takes
To arrive at the destination you set
And make your job complete

Your leave and absence hurt
Your job for me is so demanding
Where are you to reduce the load
To make the job light for me

For a month you'll be gone
For a month I'll have to wait
For your smiles and crazy thoughts
Thank God it is only a leave

Forsac D. Etogokwe

Mariana Mariana

I was moved to hot tears
When I saw her lie so still
In her snow-white garments
Many there were, men and women
Young and old, tearful folk
Sitting around still little Mariana

Her mother sat on the bare floor
Pouring tears most abundantly
And she poured forth such poetry

Then the coffin was swung in
A smart small coffin for little Mariana
Who lay un-redeemably so still

You thought she felt proud to go
As she looked neat and stiff and proud
Proud she had so irreparably gone

They picked up little Mariana
And they put her in her small thing
Her mother gesticulating like mad

She walked loudly and painfully
She spoke such pitiful words
Nobody could hold back tears

Tears were shed for the little Mariana
As she lay so still and beautiful
So sweetly beautiful in death

Fombin P.F.

Telepathy

It was a beautiful silent day
Blues skies and patches of white clouds
The sunrays came from a seventy-degree Northeast angle
Abortively striving to penetrate the gigantic compound, surrounded
With coconut and assorted fruit trees. There was absolute silence

A Negro boy stood at the gate with crossed arms, staring at the large white fence
Admiring the naturalness of the fruit trees and flowers
The birds sang their favorite seductive songs to their mates as
The Negro boy gazed, pondering whether or not to ring the doorbell
Because it was absolutely calm, quiet and silent

He was filled with love, joy and ecstasy to be there
He was also filled with agony, fright and anguish to be there
He wished his special friend would answer the doorbell as it rang
So they could share his love, joy and ecstasy as before
No one answered his call, although he was so close to happiness

The birds seized the singing as the doorbell rang continuously. It was absolutely calm,
Quiet and silent again when the Negro boy stopped ringing the doorbell
He was filled with emptiness, loneliness, agony and fright. His friend had left

He felt the pain of solitude and hoped they would meet
somewhere again.

Esendugue Greg Fonsah

My Name is Pungo

Daddy, daddy, can we accept a cat for a present?
Hell no, over my dead body, I exclaimed. And guess what
Daddy?
It is called Pungo; called Pungo? Waooh, ok we can have it
Woupi, woupi, thank you daddy, thank you, thank you

It was gentle and soft like a double Y chromosome person
With blue eyes and blend of brownish-gray color
It looked like an expensive Italian marble when lying down
With dark gray rings on its rear legs and tail

Every morning and evening it spoke to me in cat's language,
meow, meow
It will walk me to the kitchen to get coffee and to my study
room
It will lie on my books or thighs while I'm reading
It would flirt with its eyes and speak to me in cat's language,
meow, and meow

It is really called Pungo, named after my banana plantation
A dead farm later transformed into a showcase
A showcase that triggered envy, restricted reasoning moral
and
Value judgement amongst pessimists and denouncers of hard
work

It was indeed a showcase worth recognition from chronologists
And those who treasure hard work
I love Pungo my cat, although it got all the attention
I love Pungo my showcase banana plantation

Esendugue Greg Fonsah

Endnotes

Acada – refers to someone who has acquired too much academic knowledge, or the process of acquiring such education. Term often used in a derogatory manner, e.g. a bookworm or someone displaying bookish tendencies.

Akara (or makara) – bean paste deep fried in palm oil

Birocol – Bishop Rogan College, a secondary grammar school and a prep college for prospective priests, near Buea, Cameroon.

econs – Economics

Fako (Mount) – Also known as "Mount Cameroon, is a volcanic massif in southwestern Cameroon that rises to a height of 13,435 feet (4,095 meters) and extends 14 miles (23 km) inland from the Gulf of Guinea. It is the highest peak in sub-Saharan western and central Africa and the westernmost extension of a series of hills and mountains that form a natural boundary between Cameroon and Nigeria".

Da man – that man

Iroko – signifies colonialism and imperialism

Kenja – basket used for transporting produce. It is usually carried on the head

Ngeme – a village close to Mile Six Beach, Limbe (Cameroon)

Ngungu – The peak point that serves as the geographical boundary between the Anglophone and Francophone Mbo areas of Cameroon. It also served as the German military base prior to WWI.

Mens sana in corpore sano – A sound mind in a sound body

Mukala - Whiteman

Or *is the monkey right?* – stems from the Pidgin saying 'Monkey say anywhere na home – "The monkey says anywhere is home".

Osagyefo – Kwameh Nkrumah, who campaigned for a pan-Africanist state as the only viable defense against imperialism

summum bonum – virtue of the highest order

About the Authors

Epah Fonkeng is an actor and broadcaster who writes under the pen name Fonkeng E. f. In the 1980s he took to penning down "expressions of impressions formed on life's myriad ways" and as "a form of therapy" to help him recover from three tragic experiences in quick succession. Passionate about all things artistic, this former journalism lecturer has taught African dance, established a choral group, played conga and sang back-up vocals in a band, and established and served as artistic director of a drama group. His poems have been published in Canada where he lives and works as a Communications Consultant. His other works include *The Captive*, a play on the love-hate relationship between two colonial language-cultures, two books of children's stories in the Under the Baobab series, which he created, and *Thru' the Eye of a Needle* (staged at the Ottawa International Tulip Festival). He has just finished his first novel, and is currently working on another children's story book.

Esendugue Greg Fonsah, the Traditional Chief of Nshimbeng, Lebock-Mbo who holds a doctorate from the University of Nigeria, Nsukka, and a former International Corporate Executive, is an Associate Professor of Agricultural and Applied Economics at the University of Georgia, Tifton, Georgia (USA). He co-authored the *Economics of Banana Production and Marketing in the Tropics (1995)*, Minerva Press, London, recently republished by Langaa Research & Publishing CIG, Mankon, Bamenda (2012). He's also published over 300 different scientific and non-scientific journals, book chapters, bulletins, extensions, proceedings, posters and trade articles. An avid martial arts practitioner and teacher, he is also into swimming, music, golf and all aspect of football (coach, referee and active player). Poetry remains a strong passion of his with his poems having appeared in a number of anthologies in the USA including *The Best Poems of The '90s*, *The Space Between* and *The Windows of Soul*. He has travelled and worked extensively in Africa, Europe and Asia. He is married and the father of two children.

Fombin, Patrick F. holds degrees from the University of Yaounde I, Cameroon, where he is currently teaching in the Department of African Literature.

Fonge, Tembong Tobias graduated from the Department of English, University of Yaounde in 1987. He is a father of two and presently resides in Gainesville, Georgia, USA.

Forsac Amatus holds degrees in Business Administration, Mathematics and Computing Science, a post-graduate Diploma in Applied Information Technology as well as accreditation from the Canadian Securities Institute. He currently works with the Direct Investing division of TD Waterhouse Inc., in Canada, and he is the Director and co-founder of the Seven Masterminds Inc., a start-up company just founded in 2011 by business partners that are involved in varying ventures in Canada, the USA and other parts of the world. Mr. Forsac is writing another book with 6 other co-authors soon to be published in Canada titled "*Diary of the Seven Virgins*". Mr. Forsac is married and has two sons. His hobbies include sports, music and poetry.

Forsac Dorothy Etogokwe did her secondary and high school education in G. S. S. Nyasoso, Queen of the Rosary

College, Okoyong and Cameroon College of Arts and Sciences, Kumba. She later graduated from the University of Yaounde with a Bachelor degree in English Literary Studies and a Postgraduate Diploma in English Literature. She is currently an Instructor of Women and Gender Studies at the University of Buea, Cameroon, where she is a PhD candidate. She holds a combined Masters degree and a Postgraduate Diploma in Women and Gender Studies, from the University of Buea, Cameroon.

WHAT IS
TECHNOLOGY?

The who, where, why, and how!

Written by Frances Durkin

Illustrated by The Boy Fitz Hammond

FOR YOUNG READERS

Text and illustrations copyright © 2023 by b small publishing ltd. First Racehorse for Young Readers Edition 2023. 10 9 8 7 6 5 4 3 2 1 Print ISBN: 978-1-63158-714-6 Ebook ISBN: 978-1-63158-724-5

Publisher: Sam Hutchinson • Art Director: Vicky Barker • Designer: Karen Hood • Printed in Malaysia

CONTENTS

TOOLS THAT ROCK

The Stone Age is the name for the period of history from around 3.3 million years ago to 3,300 BC, when early humans and other **hominids** used rocks and stones as tools. The first stone tools were those that could be picked up and immediately used to crush, grind, or be thrown as weapons.

The earliest examples of manufactured stone tools are known as Oldowan tools. These were simple broken stones that could be used for chopping, crushing, grinding, and preparing animal skins. It is thought that these were created by *Homo habilis* and *Australopithecus.*

The tools became more advanced over time. Aechulean tools were flaked on both sides to create sharper edges. These included hand-axes, arrowheads, knives, spearheads, and **adzes**. They were made by *Homo erectus* and *Homo heidelbergensis* and could be used for hunting, preparing food, and making things.

Early stone age woman cleaning an animal skin with stone tools

Homo sapien wielding a knapped axe

---

c. 3.3 million – 300,000 years ago

Early Stone Age
Lower Palaeolithic

Early hominids, including *Homo habilis* and *Homo erectus.*

Tools for all types of tasks were made from stones.

300,000 – 40,000 years ago

Middle Stone Age
Middle Palaeolithic

Homo sapiens and Neanderthals developed techniques to make the stones into better tools.

3,300 BC

The Stone Age ends and the Bronze Age begins.

These tools are evidence of human evolution. They show how our ancient ancestors lived, hunted, and interacted with their environment.

From around 250,000 years ago *Homo sapiens* and *Neanderthals* knapped longer blades for cutting and made tiny blades called microliths that were inserted into handles. It is during this period that early cave paintings were made.

MODERN STONE TOOLS

Obsidian is a type of igneous rock that is formed when the lava from a volcano cools very quickly. It was used in the Stone Age to produce very sharp blades. Today, obsidian blades are sharper than steel but they are very brittle and can break easily. Obsidian scalpel blades are sometimes used in surgery but they are too fragile for common use.

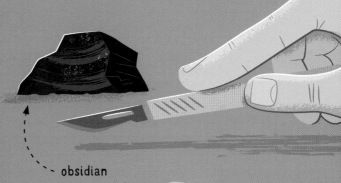

obsidian

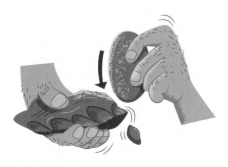

WHAT IS KNAPPING?

Knapping is the process of creating stone tools by striking a large stone, the core, with a hammerstone in order to chip off flakes. These flakes could then be knapped further to create the specific shape that was required. This method was used during the Stone Age to make all kinds of sharp-edged tools, often from a kind of stone called flint.

TAKE IT FURTHER

The Iron Age ended when the Bronze Age began. We call it the Bronze Age because there is evidence of the creation and use of bronze in the archaeology from that time.

What difference do you think this new material made to the lives of the people who lived then?

HOT OFF THE PRESS

About 600 years ago, German inventor Johannes Gutenberg created a printing press that was faster and more powerful than other machines at the time. Previous inventions inspired Gutenberg to perfect his press. These incuded **moveable type** from China, papermaking techniques from China brought to Europe by the Arab influence in Spain, durable ink from Flemish painters, and traditional wine and olive wooden presses from Roman times.

Before Gutenberg's press, monks created books by hand. This new printing press was much faster! Suddenly, it was possible to spread information far and wide.

If printing technology already existed, what did Gutenberg do differently and why did his press have such a big impact on history?

Chinese writing uses many thousands of different characters but the Latin alphabet, most widely used in books in Europe at the time, demanded just over 50 different pieces of moveable type, including upper- and lower-case letters and numerals. Gutenberg's passion for **metallurgy** resulted in the creation of a **lead alloy** that could melt and set quickly, allowing him to produce lots of pieces of very durable type.

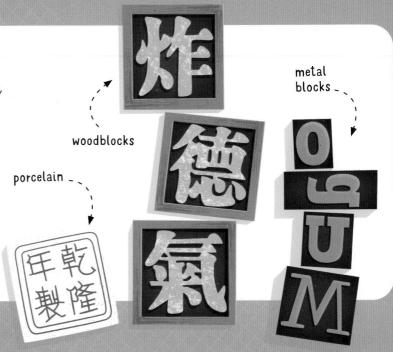

metal blocks

woodblocks

porcelain

Bi Sheng
Hubei, China

Bi Shing, a Chinese engineer, made Chinese characters from porcelain. Printers pressed ink on to paper with them. This was called moveable type.

Johann Gutenberg
Mainz, Germany

Johannes Gutenberg left Mainz for Strasbourg, now in France. Inspired by his desire to create the perfect machine, Gutenberg worked on his printing press in secret.

The **long handle** acted as a lever to press the platens together.

The **upper platen** pressed everything together.

The **lower platen** held the paper and type in place.

The metal pieces of **moveable type** carried oil-based ink, which fixed better.

Paper sat over the type. It was slightly damp to help the ink fix.

THE GUTENBERG PRESS

This new machine allowed a printer to transfer lettering from the metal type to paper using ink to create a crisp, sharp, high-quality image. When up and running, the press could produce up to 250 pages an hour.

TAKE IT FURTHER

Full name:
Johann Gensfleisch zur Laden zum Gutenberg!

- - - - - - - - - - - - - - - -

The Gutenberg Project is a digital library of over 60,000 copyright-free books.

- - - - - - - - - - - - - - - -

Information is a powerful tool. How would Gutenberg's press change things for someone living in a village or town who previously had no power or access to information? How might wealthy people use the press to get what they want?

PAINTING WITH LIGHT

In 1839 a French physicist named Louis Daguerre announced that he had invented a way of using chemicals to capture an image on a silver-plated sheet of copper. He called it the daguerreotype. Daguerre's process exposed these sheets to light, and used iodine and mercury to fix the image so that it didn't fade. Anyone who wanted their photograph taken had to remain completely still for 20 minutes!

The word photography comes from the Greek words *fos* which means "light" and *grafo* which means "to write."

---

c. AD 965 – AD 1040

Ibn al-Haytham
Cairo, Egypt

Ibn al-Haytham carried out optical experiments by projecting an image on to a screen through a hole in the wall.

1787 – 1851

Louis Daguerre
France

Daguerre invented the first practical and commercially available photographic process.

CAMERA OBSCURA

The principles behind using light to create an image had been around for hundreds of years before the invention of the daguerreotype. Around 400 BC the Chinese philosopher Mozi observed that when light from an object passed through a tiny hole it projected an inverted (upside-down) image of the original object. This was later called the camera obscura ("dark chamber") and in the nineteenth century this idea was used to create the first pinhole camera.

HOW DOES A PINHOLE CAMERA WORK?

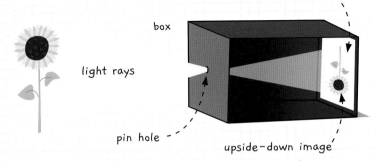

screen

box

light rays

pin hole

upside-down image

A pinhole camera is a box with a small hole in one side. When light bounces off an object and passes through the hole in the camera it forms an image of that object on the back of the box.

In modern cameras the pinhole is replaced by a lens which can allow in much more light.

pinhole camera

TAKE IT FURTHER

Build a pinhole camera!
Cut a square opening on one side of a cardboard box and tape a piece of tissue paper over the top. Use a pin to make a tiny hole on the opposite side. Cover yourself and the back of the camera with a blanket. Point the pinhole towards an object. When you look at the tissue paper you should see the inverted object appear.

1859 – 1939

Frank A. Brownell
Rochester, New York, USA

While working for the Kodak company in 1900, Brownell invented the Brownie camera. This was a small and affordable camera that became very popular with amateur photographers.

2000

Samsung released the first mobile phone with an in-built camera.

THE MAGIC OF MAKING MUSIC

Aerophones are instruments that use **vibrating** air to make sound. There are lots of different types of aerophones, from wind instruments such as flutes and clarinets to brass instruments like trumpets and saxophones.

The earliest known musical instruments are simple flutes made from swan bones and woolly mammoth ivory. They had finger holes that the musician would use to alter the sound. These instruments were found in a cave in southern Germany and are around 42,000 years old.

Flutes and trumpets became part of cultures all over the world. At first, they were mostly made from natural materials: bone, horns, wood, bamboo, or even shells. The interior spiral shape of the conch shell meant that it was used as a trumpet across the Americas, India, China, Oceania, and Europe. But ornate metal trumpets were found in the burial chamber of Egyptian Pharoah Tutankhamun who died in 1323 BC.

Playing a conch shell

HOW DOES AN AEROPHONE WORK?

The simplest aerophone is a tube which can be blown into. The addition of holes into the side of the tube means that a player can use their fingers to cover them and alter the notes. The shape and length of the tube also affects the noise that the aerophone makes.

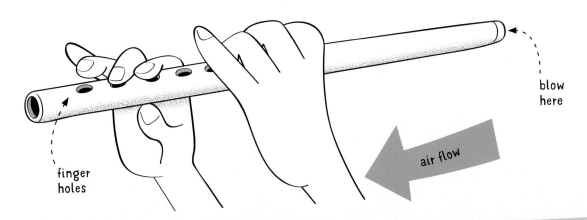

finger holes

blow here

air flow

Some aerophones use keys to help the player cover holes that are difficult to reach with one pair of hands. This **mechanism** was first invented for the flute by Theobald Boehm in the nineteenth century. Over time, new materials meant that new instruments were created in different shapes, including the clarinet, oboe, recorder, accordion, trombone, tuba, and the saxophone.

TAKE IT FURTHER

New musical instruments are being invented all the time. In 2017 Yamaha released the Venova which is a cross between a saxophone and a recorder.

Can you invent a new instrument or think of a way to change an old one?

40,000 BC

Modern-day Germany

Early modern humans made flutes from animal bones.

1324 BC

Thebes, Egypt

Beautiful instruments, such as ceremonial trumpets, were made of metal.

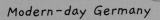

1794 - 1881

Theobald Boehm
Munich, Germany

Boehm was a musician who used his skills as a goldsmith to modernize the flute and the Boehm-system is still in use today.

FUN FACT A 43,000-year-old bone with holes was found in Slovenia in 1995 but there is a lot of debate about whether it was an instrument or if the holes were made by animal teeth.

TINY TECHNOLOGY

In the first half of the twentieth century, electronic devices such as televisions, radios, and computers contained vacuum tubes that controlled the flow of the electric current. These were big, heavy, expensive, and fragile. In 1947, a team of physicists including John Bardeen invented a smaller and more efficient way to control the electric current, called a **transistor**.

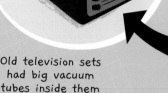

- - - a vacuum tube

Old television sets had big vacuum tubes inside them

a transistor - - -

1908 – 1991

John Bardeen
Murray Hill, New Jersey, USA

Bardeen worked on his invention with a team of colleagues.

1923 – 2005

Jack Kilby
Dallas, USA

Kilby created the integrated circuit when he combined very small electronic components on to a piece of material that conducts electricity in certain situations (a **semiconductor**). This was the first microchip.

first microchip

OUT OF THIS WORLD

These tiny and powerful microchips meant that NASA's Apollo Guidance Computer could be small and light enough to be installed on spacecrafts. They were part of the vehicles that went to the Moon.

In 1958, Jack Kilby made the technology even smaller when he invented the integrated circuit, also known as the **microchip**. The microchip contains a lot of technology, including transistors, in a very small space and meant that the machines that used them could become smaller too.

The success of the space program meant that demand for microchips grew. Today they can be found in mobile phones, smartwatches, robots, cars, and even toasters. Microchips with information are often implanted under the skin of pets so that their owners can find them if they ever get lost.

FUN FACT The engineer Gordon Moore said in 1965 that the number of transistors on a microchip would double every year. Today microchips contain billions of transistors.

TAKE IT FURTHER

Some people have suggested that humans could carry information in chips under their own skin. This could enable them to open doors or make payments with a wave of their hand.

What do you think about the possibilities for microchips?

COMPUTER COMMUNICATION

In 1962, an American scientist named Joseph Carl Robnett Licklider came up with the idea for an "Intergalactic Computer Network" that allowed computers to communicate with each other. This inspired his colleagues at the US Department of Defence Advanced Research Projects Agency (ARPA) to invent the ARPANET. It used a technology called **packet-switching** to break down messages into smaller parts and send them through telephone lines where they would reach their destination and be rebuilt. The first message was sent between computers at two different universities in California in 1969.

It was supposed to send the word "LOGIN," but the network crashed after the first two letters.

In the beginning, only a few computers could use the ARPANET but, during the 1970s, new **protocols** were written to create a massive "inter-network" link that connected computers all over the world. It was nicknamed the "internet."

During the Second World War, an inventor named Hedy Lamarr created a way to transmit radio signals across a wide range of frequencies. This **spread spectrum** technology reduced interference and made it difficult to jam or intercept signals. It became the basis for the wireless technology known as Wi-Fi that now gives us access to the internet no matter where we are.

FUN FACT The Internet of Things refers to the growing number of everyday devices such as fridges, washing machines and lightbulbs that can connect to the internet.

1915 – 1990

Joseph Carl Robnett Licklider
Arlington, Virginia, USA

At a time when computer technology was growing quickly, Licklider came up with the idea that computers should be able to share information remotely.

1914 – 2000

Hedy Lamarr
Hollywood, California, USA

Lamarr worked on her invention at the same time as being a

1955 –

Tim Berners-Lee
Geneva, Switzerland

Berners-Lee invented the World Wide Web. He released the source code for free and made the web accessible to everyone.

WHAT IS THE WORLD WIDE WEB?

When the internet first started, it was mostly used for sending emails and data files between computers. However, in 1989, a man named Tim Berners-Lee came up with the idea of using it as a place to store information that all internet users could access. He called it "Mesh" but changed the name to the "World Wide Web" and the first web page was created in 1991.

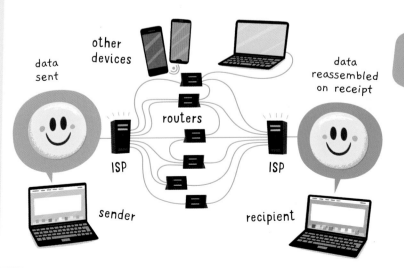

data sent

other devices

data reassembled on receipt

routers

ISP

ISP

sender

recipient

TAKE IT FURTHER

The internet is an incredible thing and the World Wide Web gives us access to endless amounts of information.

Do you think there should be any limits to what the internet can do and how people can use it?

POETRY IN MOTION

The wheel is an incredibly popular piece of engineering. Its origins are very mysterious but **archaeological evidence** shows a stone potter's wheel was used in Mesopotamia in around 3,500 BC. After that date, there is evidence of preserved wheel tracks, pictures of wheeled vehicles and toys with wheels across Asia, the Middle East, and Eastern Europe.

potter's wheel

The oldest surviving wooden wheel was discovered in Slovenia and is from around 3,000 BC. The first wheels were large and heavy solid discs of wood, eventually made lighter by the invention of **spokes** in around 2,000 BC. They were first used on horse-drawn chariots along the **Eurasian Steppe** before finding their way into Asia and Europe. These new wheels were so light and fast that chariot racing became a popular sport in parts of the ancient world.

c. 3,500 BC

Potter's wheel
Mesopotamia (modern-day Iraq)

Horizontal wheels were first used to turn clay as it was shaped into pottery.

c. 2,000 BC

Chariot Wheels
Ural Mountains, Eurasian Steppe (modern-day Russia)

Heavy wooden wheels were hollowed out to make spokes that connected the outer and inner edges.

Early tyres were made from leather and in around 1000 AD wheels were given iron **rims** to make them stronger. A very significant technological development arrived in 1846 when Robert William Thompson filled a hollow strip of **vulcanized** rubber with air and invented the first **pneumatic** tyre.

WHAT IS A WHEEL?

A wheel is a circular object that turns on an axle. It is used to make vehicles or parts of machinery move.

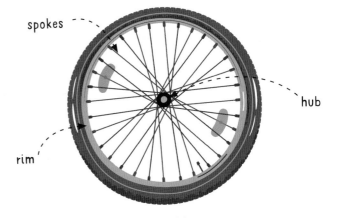

spokes

hub

rim

Wheels have lots of different uses and include spinning wheels, water wheels, steering wheels, and even the gears inside a clock are a type of wheel. Before the wheel was invented, the sled was an important method for transporting heavy items. Sleds carried heavy stones to build the pyramids, and sleds are still important today on terrains such ice and snow.

1822 – 1873

Robert William Thompson
London, England

Thompson used inflated rubber to create the kind of tire used today.

TAKE IT FURTHER

Can you improve on the wheel?

Can you think of new ways to use a wheel?

Are there any tasks that you think wheels would not help with?

MAGNETIC DIRECTION

Early travelers navigated the world using landmarks, the Sun and the stars. The compass was the first navigational tool but nobody today knows who invented it. In the eleventh century, the Chinese scientist Shen Kuo described how a **magnetized** needle suspended from a piece of silk would align itself with north and south. Before this, in China, the lodestone used to magnetize the needle was used for fortune telling and **feng shui**, not navigation, as it would point in a certain direction when left to spin on its own.

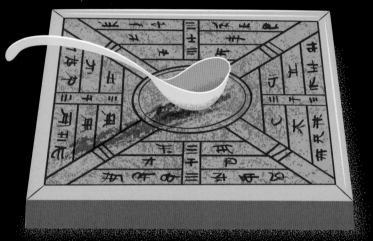

Chinese feng shui lodestone

This simple invention became widely used and, by around the year 1300 AD, the needle was suspended in a box above a compass rose that showed the cardinal points: north, south, east, and west.

box compass

HOW DOES A COMPASS WORK?

A compass is a navigational tool that uses a magnetized needle which lines up with the Earth's **Magnetic North Pole**. Magnetism was discussed by the ancient Greeks but the English physicist William Gilbert proposed, in 1600, that magnets point north because the Earth's core contains iron.

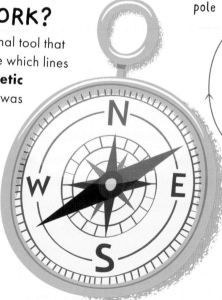

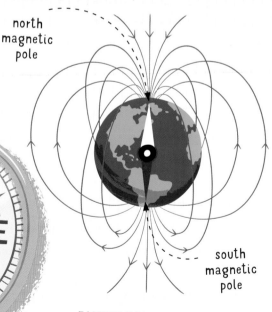

north magnetic pole

south magnetic pole

EARTH'S MAGNETIC FIELD

1031 – 1095

Shen Kuo
China

Shen Kuo was a Chinese scientist who wrote a book of essays that covered different scientific observations.

1930 –

Gladys West
Dahlgren,
Virginia, USA

West developed a computer program that used satellites to create navigation systems. Cars, planes and ships now use this to find their way to their destinations.

WHAT IS GPS?

In the early 1960s, Gladys West worked at an American naval base. She used satellites to measure the shape of the Earth and programmed a computer to work out an extremely accurate **geodetic** model of the planet. Her work became the basis of the satellite navigation system known as Global Positioning System (GPS). Today there are several other Global Navigation Satellite systems including Galileo, GLONASS, and BeiDou.

GPS satelites

Incoming GPS signal

GPS receiver

TAKE IT FURTHER

Before compasses were invented, travelers used the stars and the Sun to find their way. The Sun rises in the east and sets in the west. Can you use this to identify the cardinal directions of the compass from where you are?

At night, can you find Polaris, or the North Star?

A LIGHTBULB MOMENT

For thousands of years, humans used torches, oil lamps, candles, and lanterns to light rooms and streets. This finally changed at the end of the eighteenth century when gas lamps were invented but it was the power of electricity that completely transformed the way the world could be illuminated. The very first electric light was invented by Humphrey Davey in 1802. He passed an electric current through a platinum **filament** and made it glow. His invention wasn't very practical, but many more inventors worked on their own versions of this **incandescent light**.

Davy's first electric light

1778 – 1829

Humphrey Davy
Bristol, England

Davy's inventions led to the modern lightbulb.

1828 – 1914

Joseph Swan
Gateshead, England

Swan created a practical device that could be used safely inside homes and public buildings.

1902 – 1942

Oleg Losev
Nizhny Novgorod, Russia

While experimenting with semiconductors, Oleg Losev invented the first LED light.

In 1850, the British scientist Joseph Swan enclosed the filament inside a glass bulb. He used vacuum technology to remove the air from the bulb as oxygen would make the filament break apart. Swan continued his experiments and, in 1881, he started his own company to manufacture lightbulbs. The American inventor Thomas Edison had created his own version of the lightbulb just after Swan and the two men combined their companies to light homes and buildings all over Europe and America.

Thomas Edison's lightbulb

HOW A LIGHTBULB WORKS

When electricity passes through the filament of a lightbulb it causes it to glow. The filament in modern lightbulbs is a metal called tungsten.

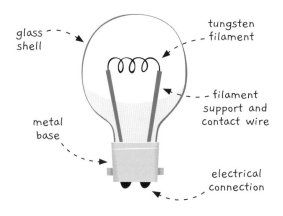

glass shell

tungsten filament

filament support and contact wire

metal base

electrical connection

The first public building in the world to be fully lit by electric lighting was the Savoy Theatre in London.

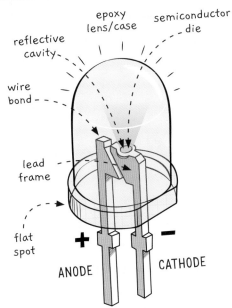

epoxy lens/case

semiconductor die

reflective cavity

wire bond

lead frame

flat spot

+ ANODE   − CATHODE

LIGHTING THE FUTURE

An LED (light emitting diode) is a tiny lightbulb without a filament. It creates light when an electric current passes through a **diode**. Russian scientist, Oleg Losev, created these in 1927. They are far more energy efficient and long-lasting than incandescent lightbulbs and are now a popular form of lighting.

TAKE IT FURTHER

Why do you think electric light was an important invention?

What do you think happened before artificial light?

PACKS OF POWER

In 1800, Luigo Galvani saw the muscles of a **dissected** frog move when he prodded them with two different pieces of metal. Galvani thought that the reaction came from the **tissue** of the animal, but his friend Alessandro Volta believed it was caused by the different metals and the liquid on the frog's legs. To test his idea, Volta placed cardboard soaked in salt water between stacked disks of copper and zinc. When the two types of metal were connected, the pile of disks created a steady electric current. The invention became known as the "voltaic pile," or the first electric battery.

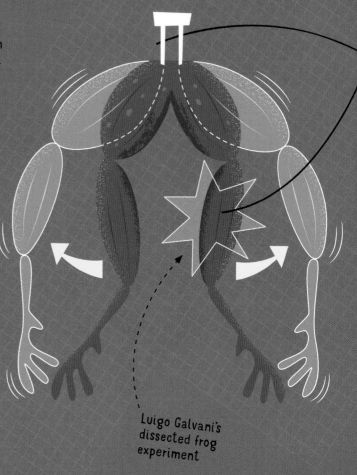

Luigo Galvani's dissected frog experiment

HOW DOES A VOLTAIC PILE WORK?

A voltaic pile, as with other batteries, contains **chemical energy** that can become **electrical energy**. The first batteries were made of a liquid substance called an electrolyte stacked together with positive and negative metal **electrodes**. The electrolyte reacted with the positive electrode to create **electrons**. The negative electrode attracted those electrons, allowing the electrons to flow and creating an electrical current.

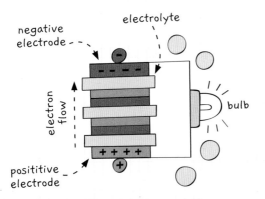

negative electrode

electrolyte

electron flow

bulb

posititive electrode

1745 – 1827

Alessandro Volta
Italy

A "volt" is now the word for a unit of electric potential.

POWERING INTO THE FUTURE

Following Volta's invention, many scientists improved upon his idea and the battery became a practical and convenient source of power. In the 1990s, research on lithium led Akira Yoshino to create the first lithium-ion battery. These rechargeable energy packs can be found in mobile phones, games consoles, and modern electric cars.

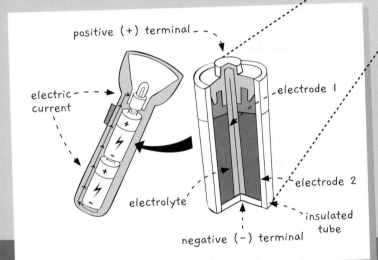

positive (+) terminal
electric current
electrode 1
electrolyte
electrode 2
negative (−) terminal
insulated tube

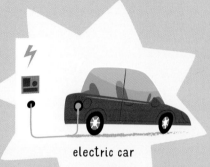

electric car

TAKE IT FURTHER

We use batteries in lots of different items around our homes.

How many things do you use that have batteries inside?

1948 –

Akira Yoshino
Kawasaki, Japan

Yoshino developed a battery that could be easily produced.

CODED COMMUNICATION

Until the early part of the nineteenth century, communicating with someone far away could take a very long time. Letters could take days, or even weeks, to reach their destinations.

In 1836, an American painter named Samuel Morse learned that it was possible to send electrical signals along a wire. He worked with Alfred Vail to create a **transmitter** that sent electrical pulses to a **receiver**. Morse invented a code of short dots and longer dashes to represent numbers. Vail expanded this to include letters and punctuation marks.

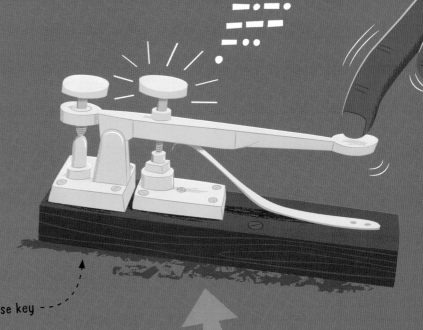

Morse and Vail's Morse key ---

1763 – 1805

Claude Chappe
Brûlon, France

Chappe's system, semaphore, needed people to use telescopes to read the signals and was quite slow.

1791 – 1872

Samuel Morse
New York, USA

Morse worked with Alfred Vail to create messages that could be received just seconds after they were sent.

WORKING WITHOUT WIRES

Developments in radio technology meant that, from the end of the nineteenth century, Morse code messages could be sent along **radio waves** instead of through wires. Guglielmo Marconi invented a radio that could transmit Morse code messages across long distances. This wireless communication was cheaper and meant that messages could be sent to ships that had no way to connect to electrograph wires.

1874 – 1937

Guglielmo Marconi
Bologna, Italy

In the mid-1890s, Marconi developed a practical radio device that that amateur radio enthusiasts still use today.

EARLY TELEGRAPHY

Methods of communicating with drumbeats, smoke, flags or lit beacons have been around for a very long time. Visual signals are called "optical telegraphy" and, in the 1790s, the Chappe brothers invented semaphore telegraphs by using rotating arms that could be moved into different positions. These were positioned on the top of towers around 15 miles apart and operators translated the message from one tower before sending it on to the next. Claude Chappe named this "semaphore."

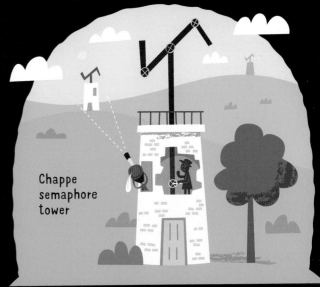

Chappe semaphore tower

FUN FACT "Telegraph" means "to write at a distance"

TAKE IT FURTHER

Can you send a Morse code message or create your own code that could be used to write a message?

IN THE MIND OF A MACHINE

Alan Turing was a mathematician who worked on machines to crack codes during the Second World War. In 1950, he wrote that computers could use information to learn how to solve problems and make decisions. A few years later this **theory** was given the name "Artificial Intelligence" (AI) and the idea has been explored by computer scientists ever since.

WHAT IS THE TURING TEST?

Turing proposed a simple test to check the intelligence of a machine. In this test, a machine and a person are asked questions by someone who doesn't know which is which. If it is impossible to tell from their answers which one is the machine, it must be as intelligent as a person. Turing predicted that the test would be passed before the year 2000. No computer has passed the Turing Test conclusively ... yet!

FUN FACT In 1846, a mathematician named Charles Babbage came up with the idea for a machine that could play noughts-and-crosses.

1912 – 1954

Alan Turing
Manchester, England

At the heart of Turing's theory is the idea that computers could learn to think for themselves.

Computer respondent   Human questioner   Human respondent

MAN VS MACHINE

Since Turing's original idea, the technology of AI has continued to be developed and tested. In the 1990s, a company called IBM built Deep Blue, a computer that was **programmed** to play chess. The ultimate test for this piece of AI was to play against the chess grandmaster and champion Garry Kasparov. In February 1996, Kasparov and Deep Blue played six games of chess. Deep Blue won the first game but Kasparov won three and the final two were draws. Kasparov was the clear winner but there was a rematch just over a year later.
This time Deep Blue won!

Since the early 2010s, AI technology has found its way into ordinary homes as digital assistants that can recognize voice commands and carry out different activities.

TAKE IT FURTHER

Artificial Intelligence is created by computer programmers.

Do you think this means that they can have human prejudices and flaws?

1995–1997

Deep Blue
New York, USA

Deep Blue was a great example of AI. Deep Blue was retired in 1997 and parts of it are now in museums.

2000s

Digital assistants change the way we live.

FASCINATING FASTENINGS

Clothes fastenings have taken many forms over thousands of years. From brooches to laces to buttons and hooks, many of them are tricky and can take time to fasten.

In 1851, an engineer called Elias Howe invented an "Automatic, Continuous Clothing Closure." This early version of the zipper was never introduced to a wide market but, forty years later, Whitcomb L. Judson created a "clasp locker." This was a guide that connected a chain of metal hooks on boots and shoes. He followed this idea with a row of hooks that were pulled together called the "c-curity." It was unsuccessful because the fastening kept bursting open.

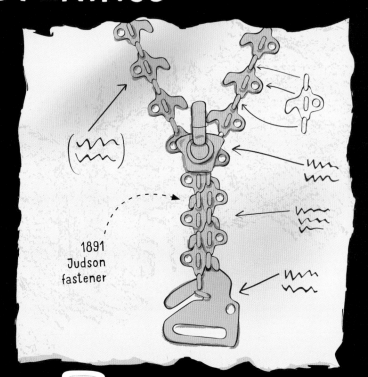

1891 Judson fastener

FROM HOOKS TO TEETH

Judson started The Universal Fastener Company and, in 1906, the company hired a Swedish engineer named Gideon Sundback. He replaced the hooks with tiny spoon-shaped rows of metal that locked together. His invention was secure and flexible, which meant that it could be used in all kinds of clothing. The company was renamed The Hookless Fastener Company.

Hook fastening zip

In 1917, the fasteners were put into money belts that became popular with the US Navy because there were no pockets on their uniforms. They soon replaced buttons on the Navy's full-body outfits called jumpsuits.

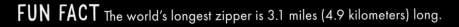

FUN FACT The world's longest zipper is 3.1 miles (4.9 kilometers) long.

Whitcomb L. Judson
Chicago, Illinois, USA

Judson showed his invention at the World's Fair in Chicago in 1893.

Gideon Sundback
Hoboken, New Jersey, USA

Sundback improved on Judson's idea.

After the First World War, the hookless fastener continued to be used and, in the 1920s, the B. F. Goodrich Company put them into their rubber boots. At the time, the word "zip" meant "move rapidly." It also sounded like the noise the hookless fastener made so the boots were named the "Zipper." Soon after they were added into children's clothes and, when they could open at both ends, they were perfect for jackets.

TAKE IT FURTHER

Think about the zips that you use. Are they on your clothes? Your backpack? Your shoes?

What are they made from?

What makes them better than other kinds of fastening such as buttons?

FUN FACT Surgical zippers use zip technology to close and protect wounds.

GLOSSARY

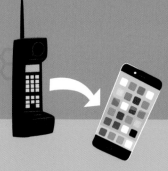

Adzes
an ancient and versatile cutting tool, similar to an axe.

Archaeological evidence
the physical objects and remains left by humans throughout history.

Chemical energy
the energy that hold atoms and molecules together. It is released when a chemical reaction takes place.

Diode
an electrical component that only allows an electrical current to flow in one direction.

Dissected
something that has been cut apart in order to be examined in detail.

Electrical energy
the power that is produced when electrons move from one atom to another.

Electrode
conductor used to make contact with a non-metallic part of a circuit.

Electron
a negatively charged subatomic particle that is found in the nucleus of an atom.

Eurasian Steppe
a huge belt of grassland that stretches from eastern Europe to China.

Feng Shui
the ancient Chinese practice of arranging furniture in order to create a balanced and harmonious environment.

Filament
a fine wire inside a lightbulb that glows when an electrical current passes through it.

Geodetic
the science of geodesy which accurately measures the Earth's shape, gravity and orientation in space.

Hominid
a member of the group of modern and extinct great apes that includes humans, gorillas, orangutans and all their ancestors.

Incandescent light
light produced when a wire (filament) is heated by an electric current.

Lead alloy
formed when lead is combined with another metal in order to give it different properties.

Magnetized
something that has been turned into a magnet.

Magnetic North Pole
the place in the northern hemisphere that compass needles point to.

Mechanism
a mechanical device for doing something. It usually refers to the parts inside a machine.

Metallurgy
the study of metals and experimenting with their various properties.

Microchip

a collection of electronic parts, including transistors, on a tiny piece of semiconductor material. This material is usually a chemical element called silicon.

Moveable type

the separate parts of a printing press with the letters on them so that they can be moved around to make different words.

Packet-switching

when small pieces of data travel quickly and efficiently through computer networks before being put back together.

Pneumatic

when compressed air is used to make something move.

Programmed

when a computer has been given the instructions to carry out specific tasks.

Protocols

a set of rules for transmitting data between computer devices.

Radio wave

a type of electromagnetic radiation with the longest wavelength.

Receiver

a device that receives electrical signals.

Rim

the outer part of a wheel.

Semiconductor

a substance that enables the control of the flow of electric current. They are commonly used in electronic devices.

Spoke

Spokes are thin rods that connect the centre (hub) of the wheel with the outer edge (rim).

Spread spectrum

a type of wireless communication which sends a message across a wide range of frequencies. This makes it more secure and reduces interference.

Theory

A theory is an idea or set of ideas based on scientific evidence that explains how something works.

Tissue

a group of cells that have similar structures and functions.

Transistor

a semiconductor device that can amplify or switch electronic signals.

Transmitter

a device that sends out radio signals.

Vibrating

when something moves rapidly back and forth.

Vulcanized

treated with chemicals and heat to make it stronger and harder.

TAKE IT FURTHER

Technology is when scientific knowledge is used to create something practical. And it's everywhere! From the wheels on a bike to the cameras in mobile phones, technology has changed the entire world. It has made it easier to communicate with each other, it has helped us to see in the dark and it has given us the tools to find our way when we are lost.

The brilliant inventors in the pages of this book have created things that we take for granted but that we often don't stop to think about. <u>Which one was your favorite?</u>

How do you use technology? What are the things that you do in a day that use technological inventions? Here are some examples:

- You read printed words in your books.
- There's a zip on your coat.
- Maybe you have batteries in your toothbrush.

The future of technology is full of exciting new ideas. It is already allowing us to explore the universe. It is helping to protect the environment. It is changing medical treatments. But what will be next?

What do you think the future holds? Can you invent something yourself? Your idea could be silly or helpful. It could be simple or complex. What is the one thing you think that technology could improve, and why?

Something you invent could have the power to make the world a better place and to change the way we work together.

<u>The possibilities are endless!</u>